The Lake District

Books by W. A. Poucher
available from Constable

Scotland
Wales
The magic of Skye
The Scottish Peaks
The Peak and Pennines
The Lakeland Peaks
The Welsh Peaks

Other books now out of print

The backbone of England
Climbing with a camera
Escape to the hills
A camera in the Cairngorms
Scotland through the lens
Highland holiday
The North Western Highlands
Lakeland scrapbook
Lakeland through the lens
Lakeland holiday
Lakeland journey
Over lakeland fells
Wanderings in Wales
Snowdonia through the lens
Snowdon holiday
Peak panorama
The Surrey hills
The magic of the Dolomites
West country journey
Journey into Ireland

Climbing the Innominate Crack on Kern Knotts, Great Gable

(frontispiece)

This well-known crack is 60 feet high on a vertical rock-face, and is a very severe ascent. Since it is a finger-and-toe problem, strong digits are essential. The climber in this picture refused to give his name or club, but did it like a cat – a superb performance.

THE LAKE DISTRICT

W.A. Poucher

Constable London

First published in Great Britain 1982
by Constable and Company Limited
10 Orange Street London WC2H 7EG
Copyright © 1983 by W. A. Poucher
ISBN 0 09 464480 2
Reprinted 1982, 1983, 1984
Text filmset by Servis Filmsetting Ltd, Manchester
Printed and bound in Japan by
Dai Nippon Company, Tokyo

The photographs

4 Climbing the Innominate Crack on Kern Knotts, Great Gable (frontispiece)
12/13 Haweswater
14/15 The head of Mardale
16/17 Small Water
18/19 Haweswater from Harter Fell
20/21 High Street and Blea Water from Harter Fell
22/23 Looking north along High Street
24/25 Helvellyn from Angle Tarn
26/27 Patterdale
28/29 The head of Ullswater
30/31 Sheffield Pike from Ullswater
32/33 Howtown
34/35 The head of Deepdale
36/37 Dovedale
38/39 Helvellyn
40/41 Striding Edge
42/43 Striding Edge from the Abyss
44/45 Windermere
46/47 Rydal Water
48/49 Grasmere
50/51 Blencathra from St John's Vale
52/53 Blencathra from Castlerigg
54/55 Crossing Sharp Edge in dense mist
56/57 The Grasmoor Fells from the Druid's Circle
58/59 Skiddaw from Bassenthwaite Lake
60/61 Friar's Crag – Derwentwater
62/63 Causey Pike from Scarfeclose Bay
64/65 Skiddaw from Ashness Bridge
66/67 Borrowdale Birches
68 Gate Crag
70/71 High Stile from Buttermere
72/73 Fleetwith Pike from Buttermere
74/75 Crummock Water
76/77 Loweswater
78/79 Grasmoor from Loweswater Church
80/81 Pillar from Ennerdale Lake
82/83 Great End from Seathwaite
84/85 On the way to Sty Head
86/87 Great End from Sty Head
88/89 Sprinkling Tarn from Central Gully Exit
90/91 Great Gable from Sprinkling Tarn
92/93 Raven Crag from Rosthwaite Fell
94/95 The summit of Glaramara
96/97 A colourful descent into Borrowdale

98/99 Buttermere and Crummock from Fleetwith
        Pike
100/101 Haystacks from Buttermere
102/103 Black Beck Tarn
104/105 The Gables from the Innominate Tarn
106/107 Pillar from the Innominate Tarn
108/109 The summit tarn on Haystacks
110/111 The Langdale Pikes from Chapel Stile
112/113 Tarn Crag from the new path
114/115 The ascent to Stickle Tarn
116/117 Legions of fell-walkers are eroding this track
118/119 Pavey Ark from Stickle Tarn
120/121 Bowfell from Gimmer Crag
122/123 Pike o'Stickle is an excellent viewpoint
124/125 Harrison Stickle
126/127 A wild day on this lofty summit
128/129 Crinkle Crags
130/131 The Scafell Pikes from Long Top
132/133 The Langdale Pikes from Blea Tarn
134/135 The Pikes from Tarn Hows
136/137 Helvellyn on the distant skyline
138/139 Wetherlam from below Tarn Hows
140/141 Pike o'Stickle from the summit cairn on
        Wetherlam
142/143 High Yewdale Farm
144/145 Dow Crag and Coniston Old Man from
        Torver
146/147 Coppermines Valley
148/149 Low Water and the Quarry Track from the
        Old Man
150/151 Walna Scar Road
    152 Dow Crag from Goat's Water
154/155 The Scafell Pikes from Grey Friar
156/157 Harter Fell from Dunnerdale
158/159 Birk's Bridge
160/161 Harter Fell from Eskdale
162/163 The summit of Harter Fell
164/165 Upper Eskdale from Harter Fell
166/167 The beginning of the walk to Upper Eskdale
168/169 Esk Pike and Bowfell from Border End
170/171 The Lakeland Giants from Border End
172/173 Wasdale Church
    174 The south window and its etching
    175 Kirkfell from the Wasdale Packhorse Bridge
176/177 The Gables from Kirkfell
178/179 The east face of the Pillar Rock
180/181 The west face of the Pillar Rock
182/183 Great Gable from Wasdale
    184 Climbing Napes Needle
186/187 Wastwater from the Sphinx Rock
    188 Great Gable from Lingmell
190/191 The Scafell Pikes from Wastwater
192/193 The precipitous face of Scafell

194/195 The summit cairn on Scafell Pike
196/197 The Screes in late afternoon
198/199 The Screes at sunset
200/201 Herding sheep in Wasdale
202/203 Wastwater on a calm afternoon
204/205 The glory of a Wasdale sunset
206/207 Sunset on the Gable

Preface

It was in Lakeland that I first discovered the charms of hill country, and it is half a century since my first visit to their delectable hills and dales. In those early days I always walked across the district, beginning with Mardale and ending with Wasdale – this was a slow progression of increasing grandeur all the way to the lofty cairn on Scafell Pike.

Of course, good weather for photography is not a common occurrence in hill country which flanks our western seaboard, where the moisture-laden winds, having crossed the Atlantic, often precipitate their contents on this landscape. The only exception to those normal conditions which I ever experienced was when I secured the photographs for my *Over Lakeland Fells*. I had allowed three months for this expedition, but the sun shone so consistently in a limpid atmosphere that I completed the walk in nineteen days. In contrast, on my visit to Lakeland in May 1981, I spent a whole month attempting to photograph the hills which, alas, were hidden day after day in a dense haze.

My photographic technique has been detailed in all my early books and updated in my four Climbing Guides, to which I refer interested readers. I have always used Kodachrome and monochrome with my two Leicas and a Leicaflex, together with a variety of lenses whose excellence can clearly be judged from the following pages.

I have written and illustrated in monochrome some thirty books which portray the magnificent scenery to be found by exploring our hills and dales – but this is only my third book in colour. I hope it will not only please my many Lakeland friends but also the thousands of readers of my pictorial guides which cover Scotland, Skye, Wales, the Peak District, and the Pennines. Readers who are interested in fell-walking and climbing will find a complete account in my *Lakeland Peaks* of the safe ascent of the hills pictured herein.

To anyone who knows Lakeland, the plan I have adopted in this book will be obvious. For those who are not so fortunate and wish to see for themselves the best of Lakeland scenery, a car will be useful, but the walks will involve a return to the starting-point where the car is parked. Nevertheless, this work will be an indispensable guide, with one scene following another across the district from east to west. Moreover, it will be clear that my greatest interest, as a mountain photographer, is in the portrayal of nature's masterpieces rather than the works of man; although a few pictures, such as those of Patterdale and Wasdale Church which have a special charm, have been included for that specific reason.

W. A. Poucher
4 Heathfield
Reigate Heath
Surrey
1981

Haweswater

This lake/reservoir lies on the eastern fringes of
Cumbria and is delightfully situated among the
hills, offering many opportunities for picture-
making.

The head of Mardale

(overleaf)

Fell-walking begins at the end of the road on the left, which may be easily reached from Glenridding or Penrith. There are several well-trodden paths leading up to all the enclosing hills, none of which presents any difficulties.

Small Water

This lovely tarn is reached during the ascent of Harter Fell by way of Nan Bield, a pass giving access to Kentmere. It is a charming place to rest awhile and enjoy the mystery and silence of our hills.

Haweswater
from Harter
Fell

(overleaf)

There are two pleasant walks to the summit of
this peak — one of them is grassy and passes
Gate Scarth en route, while the other takes in
Small Water and Nan Bield. The lofty cairn
opens up a splendid view of the lake, backed by
Cross Fell in the distant Pennines. But the water
was low when this picture was taken, so it is
marred by the exposed lateral moraines.

High Street and Blea Water from Harter Fell

The spacious view to the west from this peak
reveals a fine prospect of High Street, with Blea
Water nestling in the bosom of the green hills
below it.

Looking north along High Street

(overleaf)

A broad and lofty ridge, High Street forms an immense plateau with a conspicuous stone wall running north-south all along it. A Roman road once crossed its summit, but traces of this can only be seen when the westering sun is low. Long ago High Street was the scene of an annual fair at which horse-racing was an important feature. The narrowest part of the ridge is at the Straits of Riggindale.

Helvellyn from Angle Tarn

This beautiful sheet of water is a favourite place for picnics on a sunny day. It is passed on the descent from High Street to Patterdale, and can also easily be reached in the reverse direction.

Patterdale

This village is well known to all who visit
Ullswater, but its remarkable elevation is only
seen when it is approached from the south.

The head of Ullswater

(overleaf)

A large and beautiful lake, Ullswater has three distinct sections. From this one there is a fine view of Thornhow End and St Sunday Crag, both of which are traversed as part of the Helvellyn Horseshoe.

Sheffield Pike from Ullswater

The middle section of this lake is usually
considered its finest, with the beautiful woods
of Gowbarrow Park to the north and the slopes
of Place Fell to the south. Sheffield Pike is a
satellite of Helvellyn.

Howtown

(overleaf)

The lower section of Ullswater is a popular
venue for water-sports which are based upon
Howtown, standing at the end of a splendid
walk along the path edging the lake from
Patterdale.

The head of Deepdale

This dale, the first one on the right when driving to the Kirkstone Pass from Patterdale, does not present an attractive appearance from the road, showing only bare grassy slopes. To reach it you must walk about a mile to Wall End Cottage, beyond which the slopes to Gavel Pike and Lord's Seat fall into the dale on the right; for it is only then that this fine dalehead is suddenly disclosed. The skyline tops stretch from Hart Crag on the left to Deepdale Hause on the right; they form the precipitous eastern façade of Fairfield and are well worth exploring.

Dovedale

(overleaf)

The undulating grassy ridge of Hartsop above
How (to the right, in the picture) separates this
dale from Deepdale, and is dominated by Dove
Crag whose Y-shaped gully, a well-known rock
climb, is clearly seen from the road.

Helvellyn

One of the best-known peaks in Cumbria, and probably the most popular mountain in Lakeland, Helvellyn may be scaled by a variety of routes. The last time I was on its summit I counted more than a hundred people there, including several well-shod children under the strict control of experienced leaders. This picture shows its precipitous eastern façade, seen from Birkhouse Moor.

Striding Edge

(overleaf)

This, the most spectacular ascent of Helvellyn, is easily reached from either Glenridding or Patterdale, by well-marked paths. Care is essential when crossing its narrow rock arete, and particularly when descending the craggy Step to the saddle. Thence a rough scramble up the Abyss leads to Gough's Memorial and the summit cairn. The views down either side of the Edge are fine – even sensational.

Striding Edge from the Abyss

(overleaf pp 42/43)

The whole of the Edge is seen to advantage in retrospect: this is the classic picture of it.

Windermere

More than ten miles long, this magnificent lake is equal in volume to that of Ullswater and Wastwater together, and is twelve times that of Derwentwater. It has seen many famous boat races, and is still largely devoted to water-sports of all kinds.

Rydal Water

An unusual view of this charming lake – the photograph was taken from its eastern corner near Steps End and discloses the immense expanse of the lake, whereas only glimpses of it can be seen from the road skirting its northern shores.

Grasmere

(overleaf)

A high viewpoint near Red Bank reveals this lovely lake in its true setting, enhanced by the background of hills in which Helm Crag and Seat Sandal are prominent.

Blencathra from St John's Vale

A walk through this short but beautiful dale is
worthwhile, for just off to the left of the road
will be found one of the best packhorse bridges
in Lakeland. This photograph of it has
Blencathra in the background.

Blencathra
from Castlerigg
(overleaf)

This is a favourite belvedere for Blencathra,
with the Druid's Circle in the foreground. It is
an easy uphill stroll from Keswick, and shows
this mountain at its best.

Crossing Sharp Edge in dense mist

The most popular ascent to Blencathra's Halls
Fell Top is by way of Sharp Edge, the
narrowest and most sensational rock ridge in
the district.

The Grasmoor Fells from the Druid's Circle

(overleaf)

Another shot from this coign of vantage (see page 52/53), with a distant background of the Grasmoor Fells. Of course, the fine clouds make the picture.

Skiddaw from Bassenthwaite Lake

This lake has never achieved distinction
because, unlike most of the others, it lacks a
fine mountain dalehead. Nevertheless, it is a
picturesque sheet of water and yields a good
view of Skiddaw from its northern outflow.

Friar's Crag –
Derwentwater

(overleaf)

This is one of the best-known and best-loved scenes in all Lakeland. From the point of view of the photographer, it not only requires a brilliant sunny morning but also a windless day and a still lake to secure a reflection with a clear outline of Causey Pike in the background. The seats at the end of the crag are a favourite with the elderly, who sit there for hours enjoying the serenity of the view.

Causey Pike from Scarfeclose Bay

A special favourite of mine, this secluded inlet
does not attract the crowds. It is always a
pleasure to rest on its shore and recall the
splendour of the Central Fells, whose distant
summits appear above the Jaws of Borrowdale.

Skiddaw from Ashness Bridge

(overleaf)

This scene is especially attractive when the tapestry of autumn colours leads the eye to the blue of Derwentwater and the noble form of Skiddaw. It has a special appeal for all walkers bound for Watendlath.

Borrowdale Birches

This charming dale has always been famous for
its birches; in this picture they are dominated by
Gate Crag and Knitting How.

Gate Crag

A fine mountain view, with the crag seen at its best from a sharp bend in the river, just beside the busy road.

High Stile
from Buttermere

(overleaf)

One of the finest walks in this enchanting valley is the complete traverse of the High Stile range of hills, which rise on the south-western side of Buttermere. The fine trees at its head have always attracted photographers.

Fleetwith Pike
from Buttermere

(overleaf pp 72/73)

A grey day and still lake reflecting the mountains always make a good picture. The only problem is to be there when these conditions prevail.

Crummock Water

The road on the right twists past the narrows of this lovely lake and requires special care by motorists, owing to the frequent passing of large coaches. In late autumn the colours here are superb.

Loweswater

This, the third lake in the Buttermere valley, is
seen at its best from its western end, but access
to this viewpoint is now difficult and the
marshy ground very wet underfoot. It opens up
a fine prospect of the massive Grasmoor Fells.

Grasmoor from Loweswater Church

(overleaf)

A beautiful church in such a secluded spot comes as a surprise, but it makes a good foreground for Grasmoor, one of the finest belvederes and least-climbed peaks in Lakeland.

Pillar from Ennerdale Lake

Ennerdale is a very long valley – it seems
endless when the rain pours down on the tired
fell-walker. The finest scene, unfolded at its
western end, is that of Pillar, with just a
glimpse (on its left, and behind it) of the
famous Pillar Rock.

Great End
from Seathwaite

(overleaf)

A popular walk to the Central Fells starts from the hamlet of Seathwaite. Great End is the highest peak to be seen, and is less well known than Scafell Pike and Great Gable, which are both equally accessible – for that very reason, it is a good one to make for.

On the way to Sty Head

After passing Stockley Bridge the hard work
begins, but when you reach the 1,000-ft
boulder, the wild, rocky valley flattens out, as
seen in this picture, and progress becomes
easier. One of the most charming sections of
the valley has this cascading stream, with the
Scafell Pikes looming on the far horizon.

Great End from Sty Head

(overleaf)

Great End is seen to advantage from a point just beyond the cairn on Sty Head. The great ravine of Skew Gill splits the face of the mountain, and its ascent makes a sporting route to the summit.

Sprinkling Tarn from Central Gully Exit

The flattish top of Great End is immense, and
is strewn with boulders and cairns. From its
northern edge the finest views are revealed; one
of them is shown in this photograph, with
Sprinkling Tarn lying more than a thousand
feet below.

Great Gable from Sprinkling Tarn
(overleaf)

This small sheet of water is one of the most beautiful in the district, and is beloved of all fell-walkers who pause here to enjoy the wild scene.

Raven Crag from Rosthwaite Fell

The western wall of Comb Gill is supported by
Raven Crag (centre), which is a climbers'
playground. In the background looms Great
Gable. This viewpoint is part of the route to
Glaramara by way of Rosthwaite Fell, which is
crowned by Bessy Boot – a curious but
romantic name for its summit.

The summit
of Glaramara

(overleaf)

Many lovers of Lakeland consider this peak one
of the finest in the district because it unfolds
such an immense panorama in all directions.
This picture looks to the north, where
Derwentwater is backed by Skiddaw in the far
distance.

A colourful descent into Borrowdale

The easiest way down from Glaramara is by
Thornythwaite Fell. The colours of the
landscape beyond in late autumn are in striking
contrast to the barren rock and scree of the
open fell.

Buttermere and Crummock from Fleetwith Pike

(overleaf)

A view is not always improved by a lofty vantage-point, but in this case Fleetwith Pike yields a superb vista of the valley and its lovely lakes.

Haystacks from Buttermere

I have often been asked which is the most beautiful hill in Lakeland, and have no hesitation in choosing Haystacks, 1,750 ft high and surrounded by a ring of higher peaks. It is easily reached from the car-park on Honister, but a more interesting approach is the walk from Warnscale Bottom. On approaching the plateau, the track, running through heather, passes three lovely tarns by which one may sit and enjoy, in silence, the beauty of one of nature's masterpieces.

Black Beck Tarn

This is the first tarn encountered in the
delightful walk to Haystacks, and the picture
catches the sombre aspect which it so often
presents.

The Gables from the Innominate Tarn

(overleaf)

A rough scramble now follows, and the second
lake, the Innominate Tarn, suddenly appears
ahead, its surface usually reedy but reflecting the
Gables on a calm day.

Pillar from the Innominate Tarn

(overleaf pp 106/107)

Turning to the right, the path keeps to the
shore of the Tarn, with Pillar, dominating the
scene, in the background.

The summit tarn on Haystacks

The third tarn comes as a surprise, lying in a rocky basin on the summit. From here there is a fine distant view of the Grasmoor Fells.

The Langdale Pikes from Chapel Stile

(overleaf)

Who has not stopped in surprise and admiration on seeing for the first time the superb profile of this group of hills? The sight of them on a clear day immediately induces the urge to climb them, and they may be ascended from any side without difficulty. The two most popular routes start at the New Dungeon Hotel; one goes by Mill Gill and the other by Dungeon Ghyll. Both of them are delightful – my advice is to ascend by one and descend by the other.

Tarn Crag from the new path

Because of erosion, the original path by Mill Gill to the Langdale Pikes has had to be abandoned. This top is the first to be seen from the new path, which runs uphill beside a chattering beck.

The ascent to Stickle Tarn

(overleaf)

The new path goes to-the left, near the prominent waterfalls, and later emerges on the shore of Stickle Tarn.

Legions of fell-walkers are eroding this track

Erosion is a serious problem on the most
popular tracks, and the new path is already
showing signs of wear.

Pavey Ark from Stickle Tarn

(overleaf)

This magnificent crag dominates the tarn and is a favourite of the rock climber. Rising diagonally from right to left is the narrow track known as Jack's Rake, a sensational, exposed route of ascent which should be severely left alone by all fell-walkers.

Bowfell from Gimmer Crag

While Bowfell Peak in the background may be
climbed by anyone who is fit, the almost
vertical Gimmer Crag in the foreground is
reserved for rock climbers.

Pike o' Stickle is an excellent viewpoint

(overleaf)

Pike o' Stickle stands high and precipitously above Mickleden, and on a clear day it rewards the walker with a wide panorama, extending from Harrison Stickle right round the western arc to the Gables. Below is the well-known track up Rossett Gill to Ewer Gap and Esk Hause.

Harrison Stickle

The horizontal summit of this peak is only a
short step from Pike o' Stickle, but as it is only
2,401 ft high, the views it unfolds are restricted
by the higher encircling fells.

A wild day on this lofty summit

(overleaf)

I shall always remember the day I took this picture because, as indicated by the immense cloudscape, there was a terrific wind which made it difficult to stand up, let alone keep still when making the exposure. As the sharpness of this study shows, I eventually succeeded.

Crinkle Crags

This rocky ridge separates Great Langdale from Upper Eskdale, and so reveals the hills on either side. There are several easy walks to its summit ridge, which is popular with old and young alike. But the most sporting ascent is by Crinkle Gill, which starts at the footbridge in Oxendale where the Gill is only a short step to the left. It is for the experienced fell-walker only, but should on no account be entered when the stream is in spate.

The Scafell Pikes from Long Top

(overleaf)

Long Top is the highest Crinkle and is an excellent place from which to appraise the Lakeland Giants. Together with Bowfell, these encircle the remote wilds of Upper Eskdale.

The Langdale Pikes from Blea Tarn

(overleaf pp 132/133)

This beautiful tarn lies beside the narrow hill-road connecting Great and Little Langdale. To see it smooth as a mirror means an early visit, before the wind has ruffled its surface. For this shot I had to lie down on the tarn's edge, otherwise there would have been no foreground.

The Pikes from Tarn Hows

It is unusual to visit this beauty-spot and find
no one else there, but this happened to me once
on a cold and snowy day in February. During
the summer season it is usually crowded, for it
undoubtedly merits a visit by any passing
traveller. This picture, taken near the Tarn
Hows outflow, shows in the distance the
Langdale Pikes.

Helvellyn on the distant skyline

(overleaf)

Photographing Tarn Hows with the longer stretch of water in the foreground reveals the Helvellyn range on the horizon.

Wetherlam from below Tarn Hows

The splendid ridge of Wetherlam is seen in its
entirety from the road leaving these tarns.

Pike o' Stickle from the summit cairn on Wetherlam

(overleaf)

From Coniston it is a long walk to this splendid viewpoint, with a remarkable change in terrain along the way. This occurs at Lad Stones, which also yields a spectacular view of Swirl How and its satellites.

High Yewdale Farm

Of special interest at this farm is the Spinning
Gallery on the wool barn, possibly the best
preserved example of its kind in Lakeland.

Dow Crag and Coniston Old Man
from Torver

(overleaf)

Both of these tops are of interest; Dow Crag to
the rock climber and Coniston Old Man to the
fell-walker. The Old Man is probably one of the
most popular ascents in Lakeland, and many
climbers, on attaining the summit, try to pick
out Blackpool Tower in the vast panorama!

Coppermines Valley

This scene will be familiar to all who ascend the
Old Man, for the white building is a well-
known youth hostel. Varied routes from its
doors give access to any section of the ridge, as
far north as Carrs.

Low Water and the Quarry Track from the Old Man

(overleaf)

It is a pleasant experience to look down on the track you have climbed to this summit, once the hard work has been done.

Walna Scar Road

This is perhaps the best walk in the Coniston
Fells, yielding views of their outstanding
features all the way over the watershed and
down into Dunnerdale.

Dow Crag from Goat's Water

These towering cliffs were some of the first in Lakeland to attract the rock climber, and they have since been explored in detail.

The Scafell Pikes from Grey Friar

(overleaf)

There are many different places on the Coniston Fells from which to enjoy the view of these Pikes, but artist and photographer have long agreed that Grey Friar is the finest belvedere of them all.

Harter Fell from Dunnerdale

This valley contains no lake and so is often
neglected by the visitor. But in the late autumn
Dunnerdale is one of the loveliest and most
colourful in the whole of Lakeland.

Birk's Bridge

Fell-walkers always halt awhile when they reach
this well-known bridge, and in warm weather
post a lookout on top of it and then take off
their clothes to enjoy a swim in the deep pool.

Harter Fell
from Eskdale
(overleaf)

One of the hills that characterize the lower stretches of this valley is Harter Fell. It may easily be climbed from almost every side, but its rocky summit is the only one in Lakeland that cannot be reached without the use of the hands.

The summit of Harter Fell

Here is a picture of that rocky summit, with my
son by the cairn.

Upper Eskdale from Harter Fell

(overleaf)

The Penny Hill route to the summit of this peak opens up many beautiful views of the hills, and this picture was taken from the best viewpoint of them all. The farm of Brotherilkeld lies in the valley below, and the horizon is ringed by all the high tops, from Scafell to Long Top on the Crinkles.

The beginning of the walk to Upper Eskdale

There are few climbers who have not revelled
in this walk which passes many points of
interest, including the Esk Falls and the source
of the beck in the remote fastnesses of the
dalehead.

Esk Pike and Bowfell from Border End

(overleaf)

I first discovered this excellent viewpoint as long ago as December 1939, when my son and I spent a fortnight walking over the western fells. I return to it every time I drive over Hardknott Pass, as Border End is only 500 ft above the summit of the pass and, in my opinion, reveals the finest panorama in all Lakeland.

The Lakeland Giants from Border End

(overleaf pp 170/171)

This is the best shot I have ever taken of this dramatic scene. It was in late October, when the colours of the landscape were at their best, and a strong westerly wind sweeping over the hills brought clouds whose moving shadows imparted a special grandeur to the highest mountains in Lakeland.

Wasdale Church

This is one of the smallest churches in England
and is also famous for the etching of Napes
Needle on its south window. Climbers who
have fallen to their death on the surrounding
hills have been buried beside it, in the shadow
of the encircling yews.

The south window and its etching

(overleaf)

The etching of Napes Needle, with the Biblical quotation beneath it which sums up the sentiments of all climbers, are often missed by visitors to this church.

Kirkfell from the Wasdale Packhorse Bridge

(overleaf p 175)

Reaching the summit of this mountain presents no problem, but for some strange reason it is one of the few hills that seldom draw the fellwalker. There are two summit cairns from which to see the surrounding hills; the view of the Scafells above Lingmell in the late afternoon is one of the best.

The Gables from Kirkfell

(overleaf pp 176/177)

After walking down Kirkfell summit plateau, with its two tiny tarns, this view of the Gables comes as a surprise: it has lost all the splendour of its pyramidal elevation as seen from Wasdale (page 182/183).

I WILL LIFT UP MINE EYES
UNTO THE HILLS
FROM WHENCE
COMETH MY
STRENGTH.

The east face of the Pillar Rock

The high-level route to the summit of Pillar
Fell is the most interesting approach, because at
the end of it stands Robinson's Cairn which
discloses the east face of this formidable
climbers' playground.

The west face of the Pillar Rock

(overleaf)

Reaching the viewpoint for this study entailed a steep and rough descent directly from the summit of the mountain. Pillar Rock can only be photographed to perfection on a sunny afternoon in summer, for at other times it is dimmed by the shadow of the peak.

Great Gable from Wasdale

(overleaf pp 182/183)

Probably the shapeliest mountain in Lakeland, Great Gable is prominent in all the views from Wastwater. Making a satisfactory picture of it requires lighting that will clearly reveal the Napes Ridges below the summit – I took this shot at 7 p.m., near Wasdale Church, when the sky cleared briefly after a typical stormy Lakeland day.

Climbing Napes Needle

Fell-walkers who wish to see – rather than climb – this famous Needle should ascend the gully below it and scale the easy rocks on the left to reach the Dress Circle. Here they will find seats for quite a few people.

Wastwater from the Sphinx Rock

(overleaf)

This remarkably shaped rock will be found at the end of the traverse, and the stance for this photograph needs a steady head. It is a risky place in which to change a camera lens, as there are steep slopes below of about 1,500 feet.

Great Gable from Lingmell

In my early days it was rare to see another climber on Lingmell, which is only a short step from the Corridor Route to Scafell Pike. But after the publication of several of my photographs taken from it, climbers began to realize its excellence as a viewpoint, and especially for a dynamic shot of Great Gable, in which Napes Ridges and the ascending track to Sty Head are prominent.

The Scafell Pikes from Wastwater

(overleaf)

These well-known peaks are seen to advantage from the upper reaches of the lake: from left to right they are Lingmell, Scafell Pike, and Scafell. Brown Tongue rises along the valley below them and is a seemingly endless slog up to Hollow Stones, seen middle distance, centre – one of the most impressive places in this group of hills.

The precipitous face of Scafell

The cliffs seen in this photograph rise to hem in
the south side of Hollow Stones, and have
played an important part in the history of rock
climbing. But as they face the north, the sun
only catches them at dawn, and late on a
summer day.

The summit cairn on Scafell Pike

This peak is the highest in Lakeland, so
attaining its cairn is the ambition of all fell-
walkers. On a clear day the rewards of
conquering it are immense; on one memorable
occasion I saw not only Snae Fell on the Isle of
Man, but also an aeroplane flying towards it.

The Screes in late afternoon

(overleaf)

These Screes are unique in Britain, and the millions of stones falling into Wastwater make an impressive picture. They are flanked on the right by several gullies which occasionally attract the rock climber, and, facing north-west, are poorly illuminated till late in the day.

The Screes at sunset

(overleaf pp 198/199)

The marvellous transformation, as the setting sun reaches them, has to be seen to be believed.

Herding sheep in Wasdale

A lucky shot, only possible in late autumn.

Wastwater on a calm afternoon

(overleaf)

This superb lake is frequently seen by visitors, but this view of its mirrored surface may come as a surprise – not only are its waters often ruffled, but sometimes one can see neither them nor its enclosing hills.

The glory of a Wasdale sunset

(overleaf pp 204/205)

This photograph catches a marvellous scene at its best, but I have to confess that it was the only time I have ever seen it like this!

Sunset on the Gable

I actually met the earth's shadow on this late
descent of the Gable.